Landlocked:
Etymology of Whale-Fish and Grace

poems by

Danèlle Lejeune

Finishing Line Press
Georgetown, Kentucky

Landlocked:
Etymology of Whale-Fish and Grace

GRATEFUL ACKNOWLEDGMENTS

Literary Mama: *Midday in Spring, Poppy's Daughter, From the cab of the farm truck in Spring, Woman's Work*
Red River Review: *Daughter of the Osmanthus River*
Whale Road Review: *What Brings Her Ghost Back*
Red Paint Hill: *Etymology of Whale-Fish, Lorraine's Blue Bottle Blues, Glacial Remains*
MothersAlwaysWrite: *Four Words*
Rose Red Review: *Bone People*
Glass Poetry Journal: *Every Delicate Step*
Nottingham Review: *I'll Tell You*

Thank you to the folks at Ossabaw Writers' Retreat, Charles University, and the Vermont Studio Center for your guidance and mentorship. Special thank you to Tony Morris, Neil Shepard, James Ragan, Beverly Donofrio, Carol Roh, Lenore Hart, and David Poyer for your mentorship and encouragement. An alligator has unstuck my life.

Publisher: Leah Maines
Editor: Christen Kincaid
Cover Art: Danèlle Lejeune
Author Photo: Danèlle Lejeune
Cover Design: Elizabeth Maines McCleavy

Printed in the USA on acid-free paper.
Order online: www.finishinglinepress.com
                also available on amazon.com

Author inquiries and mail orders:
Finishing Line Press
P. O. Box 1626
Georgetown, Kentucky 40324
U. S. A.

Table of Contents

Dedicated to Dandelions,
the alligator at Ossabaw,
and my children.

Becoming a Skin Walker is a Curse:

Part 1

Bembix, B. americana.:
Little White Bees

Part I

In Catechism class, we read
about Saint Rita, whose infant
body was swaddled with a swarm
of white bees, unstung

she slept sweetly as they went in
her mouth, tickled her delicate
dreaming eyelids, the local priest in awe,

declaring a miracle. She, the saint
of beaten women, loving mothers,
of impossible dischord, prayed

and saved her own sons'
immortal souls with dysentery,
fell the town mayor with black
plague, and brought peace.

White bees, they whisper,
are messengers of God.
A miracle is coming, disguised
as misery or sting.

Part II

Little white bees? my daughter gasps,
points to the thyme
their snow down fur,
ice wings humming.

Yes, love, I whispers back,
Saint Rita's bees are sand wasps.
Look at their bodies and how they dance.

They are not like other bees,
clinging to gold powder, rolling
through flower heads and thyme leaves,
bumbling home, overfed and drunk
but focused on their task,

the sand wasp is flesh
eater, preys upon lacewings,
cluster flies, small beasts
drawn to sweet blossoms,

She takes the stung carcasses
back to her sandy retreat,
a feast for the brood
wrapped in comb and jelly,

nest holes nestled in the sand,
deep, so birds of the sea
cannot reach in and snatch.

These are not like other bees,
girl. Not sweetlings. Not fragile.
Look at how she looks at us, not a drop of fear.

Part III

My daughter, still as the tall grass,
listens, smile twitching
the corner of her lips, she remembers
in dreams the taste of bees.

She sings, her breath carried
on the air, a flutter and buzzing
of delicate wings, *Blessed Saint Rita,*
hear our prayers and deliver us, save us.

Woman's Work

The tractor and hay baler stuck and broken,
leaving her with blade and hot afternoon sun,
swinging the scythe back and forth through
tall grass, clearing a path for the electric fence.

That same fence that yesterday shorted out, and she chased
and rounds up pigs from the road, hen house,
neighbor's orchard, hauling them home
in the trailer with the bad tire and rusting floor.

*Soon enough robots will do a million other things
we can't even conceive of*, she thinks, and sets the blade down,
sips the warm water and listens for her children playing
near the house. Checks for blisters on her hands,

swings the blade again, bruised shoulder aching,
one misstep, a slice through flesh,
tendon, bone—the backhand of a misspoken word,
breeze rises from the north, tieback hair falling,
undone. Shhhhh, swish, shhhhh,
and lifting, stepping forward, repeat, again,

Soon enough robots will do a million other things—
the children are suddenly quiet, the sky shadowing, a storm eclipsing,
the wind shifting, lifting the ragweed stalks and cut prairie grass,
pollen sticking to flesh, eyelashes, sending bird to the trees,

setting the blade-end deep into ground, leaning
on the handle and watching the clouds turn, swirling.
In song and myth, sky and the earth are woman, mother,
but this storm feels like his truck
driving too fast on the road home.

Rooster Gumbo

My grandma used to squint
her eyes and tell me stories
about skin walkers in the swamps,
giant panthers who'd slip off their fur
and walk as women, naked
knee-deep, bare-footed
through brackish water
digging claws into the bald
knees of cypress, and stretch
out bodies, lithe and warm,
howling for something more
than lust and blood.

She would remind me,
when I stole red lipstick
and a handful of glass marbles
from the Ben Franklin
and again when she found me outside
one morning, a pack of my mother's
Virginia Slims in my pocket, tongue
slurring fuck you's and cunt words,
a feral child drunk on the swingset,
a blur of fire ants and kicking,
that becoming a skin walker is a curse.

But these women, who throw back
whiskey straight up,
fists fly and blood runs hot,
who will chase you down
crush bone when you done wrong?
That's who I want to be.

Women who hide fire
and flood behind their eyes,
a flash of everything, stir
the pot, child, so the roux don't burn,
now, and the pot simmers.

Their black fur falling to the ground,
or hung on kitchen chairs, loosely.

These are the women she warned of,
the women I dreamed and feared.
Red high heels, pearls at their throats,
cherry-stained lips as they dance
on the gnarled knees of the trees,
waiting for a bedtime story
of heartbreak to match their own.

Tell me punishment
will fall on me for passion and greed,
wanting what's not mine,
for leaving you and you loving me.

Grandma says, *Shhhhh child, now eat.*

Pestsäule

Thousands of bees
wrap around the folds
of Mary's gown, swarm
the base of the monument,
cover sculpted faces
of children lost to the plague.

Something in the wind
set this hive to swarm,
brought them to this gravestone
for the dead,
legs yellow, sticky
from milkweed pollen
that now holds them
like glue, to the Virgin,

cover her with gold dust,
fill the eyes and open mouths
with buzzing wings. Multitudes
of bees. A universe
of bees.

Parish Blues

Muddy and slow
        like a breeze on the bayou
on a
hot
       august morning
just
       before the sun turns
                     violent
and
       our swamp goes quiet
       in the heat.
Like the time I stood
in Mo Mo's back
yard
       in the middle
       of the night
fearless
until someone saw
me from the house
called out
             about rattlesnakes….
       rattlesnakes all around me
               in the leaves
       cottonmouths.

Don't move.

Selkie Moves to Iowa

We come from sea-cliffs, iron
and salt in our flesh, Nordic scourges,
Catholic inquisitions, fisher's hooks.

Lovers caught in the tide's pull,
blood spilled on land's dark quilt.

Put your hand here. Lower.
Damp and tangled in linen sheets.
Human hunger, a dark flavor bitter.
Now, feel. The kick. The heartbeat.

In the morning, I rise, step
out, alone. Damp
footprints on the porch, mid-summer.

I close my eyes. Smell the dry breeze, dusty
gravel, prairie grass. Afternoon sun,
hot on my skin, cotton blouse
clinging, wet. Iron and salt in my flesh.

Every Delicate Step

The laughter
crushed on rocks
and bone   still
rings in my

ears, pearls and
silver   bells,
with every
        delicate
step—*Disgrace,*

she whispers
and   the soft
slide of her
sssss,   tickles
down my throat.

Wall Clouds

Sharp shelf of clouds rolls
on the horizon, heavy,
low over the hills, the rain,
sheets of black, silver above
the old barn as the rumble
passes through my breath,
down into marrow.

Across the field, a farmer races
the storm with the cultivator,
old machine used parts, weaker
welds where the work
has broken them over and over.

Here I stand on the hill, wind in my hair,
the chickens in the yard still
playing, they don't care that the funnel
clouds form overhead, they know
there is nothing they can do, the storm
comes anyway and the rain.

Sheet and linen left out between
two t-posts on a fraying rope line,
rusty-springed clothespins holding—
this wind tests their make and metal.
Tonight, the sea and the song
collide in the sky,
grass in the pasture laid flat,
while heavy rain and straight-line
winds break branches from the old oaks,
lightning-flashed,
fire-burnt sycamore crashes down,
snapped under pressure and age
as we shelter in the damp
basement with the failing foundation,
strain to hear the radio
signal, tell us it is safe

even though we still hear
water rising and the rumbling.

Our daughter cries, a cherished
tricycle left in the yard,
bell and streamers already crushed,
we hold each other tight, let fear
take us. Tonight we can't relax,
instead tell ghost stories in the darkness,
remember just for a moment, love,

the grass will shed the damp, slowly
rise, tall and slender
and dance, sway in the warm breeze
knowing as only grass does
how rain soaks the soil.

Lorraine's Blue Bottle Blues

I was told early that ghosts would crawl
into Lorraine's blue bottles, placed upside
down on fence posts and crape-myrtle branches.

Longing fell, a shawl around her shoulders, tangled,
long dishwater hair, lingerie dropped to the planked
floors when no one was looking, negligee a regret.

Splinters marked the floors where the wax wore off.
A simple woman, spilling salt in thresholds.
What haints lingered here stopped at that white line,

scared of her blue eyes? Giving her forever a home.
Salt and red clay tracked in, staining wood, streaked
like blood dragged heavy through.

I have these worn out shoes, and tiny forget-me-nots
fell out the toes as we danced in the kitchen, blue on the waltz
I swayed and twirled as I passed through each step.

Grains of salt are still here, and here.
Cross my heart. Lorraine holds her ear to the bottle.
I whisper, *Let me go. Let me go.*

From the cab of the old farm truck on the first day of spring

This day begins pulling stillborn lambs from a bloody sheep,
grateful and tired, I hold her head and tell her she is not alone.
I know what it is like to have stuck babies
pulled from my body, with a calf jack and chains.

I hoist up into the old truck, pull the seat forward
to see what is in front of me,
worry that driving the truck into the tall dry grass
will set everything on fire,
spread over the hills before it swallows us too.

The day moves on, I tend to the sore and bleeding ewe,
carry the limp bodies of her stillbirth,
in an orange bucket to the edge of the woods,
bury them shallow with much reverence
to the darkness that settles on the farm.

The sun was soon high in the sky when I remember
breakfast and the children still in pajamas.
I set out strawberries and milk, sandwiches later.
They play in the yard with escaped piglets and chickens,
all unaware that death has visited and carried off
so much of my heart this morning.

The first day of spring, the first warm day,
the maples drip drip dripping sap into buckets.
From that sweetness we will get sugar drunk
and laugh over the children's stories at dinner.
We will wash blood and mud from our boots, listen:
the rustle of the winter grass in the warming breeze.

Midday in Spring

Plastic wrap, the bloody,
crumpled clearfoil lies on
the counter dripping meat blood
pooling in swirls of
reds and browns.

I am searing meat in the hot skillet
for just another meal, vegetables and spices,
starch to expand.

The cat jumps up, dirty paws
to lick and lick and leave
bloody meat juice paw prints
across the kitchen floor.

I stir.
The wooden spoon
warms as I caramelize,
crisp, sweet on the inside,
cayenne and aleppo and thyme,
kick my rib cage
like my own heart beating a lie.

My children are playing.
I am a ghost to them, they pretend
my calling to them is the wind in the trees.
They climb higher to escape.

I watch through windows,
catching glimpses through branches and sunlight.
Their laughter windchimes in the warm breeze.
Steam hisses from the pot and I turn,
wooden spoon churning the stock.

It is almost time.

Poppy's Daughter, A Eulogy

Poppy, *Fast Eater*, as my small daughter called you.

You were my midwife as you lambed that first spring,
green curling up and out from the ground.
Three children had been ripped from my belly
under the heat of surgical glare
and the sleep offered by chemical cocktails.
I had never seen a live birth.

But you knew how to drop
a lamb, turn and bring life
into the wet mewing shiver,
soft in the hay, scared of the cold, harsh air
of this world, lift up, spill milk
into the mouth of lambs.

And later, you stood between us and the the wolves
and feral dogs that ran the highways on the edge of our pastures,
and wet nursed lambs the other ewes rejected
who'd have starved and fallen to coyotes and buzzards without you.

How could I dare milk you to make cheese?
How could I take from you your birthright?
We never could eat your lambs, your daughters standing by your side,
our own royalty of Poppy.
How could I not know you'd die
broken-hearted when we put down our cow, Rosie,
blizzard coming, leg broken, pistol to her head?

Cowering when I brought you water in the afternoon thaw,
asking us why, why, why?
Pleading.
What is mercy?

The Last Swarm

I watched them for hours, the heart of a swarm,
the humming scent of the pear blossoms,

the only bees that ever stung me, so angry the box shifted,
frames spilling under the weight of their grievances,

souring the honey, larvae dying in the brood cells, milky-
white turning grey, and the stand gave out. I braced

the brood boxes, sistered and screwed two by fours.
Nothing held. The whole thing collapsed—bees rising

in a cloud from their broken home, covering shoulders
and torso. I held my breath, closed my eyes waiting

for their anger to flow through, stung here and here,
my pregnant belly, the only place my suit wouldn't tie.

Hearts pulled out. Then, they settled, rose up
with the queen, leaving the honey to ferment and rot

in frames, dead bees and mites littering the boxes,
as they drifted to a young pear tree, blossoms opened,

the too sweet pollen shaken off, where the weight
of the swarm bent the limb, just within my reach,

where I could—bring them home.
But this day, I let go.

Every Breaking Wave:

Part 2

Bone People

We feed tooth and maul,
bang out tunes on ivory keys,
pick cotton bolls
with wishbones and sorry
glances across the work,

sharpen scythe and axe
to cut through flesh and tendon,
green fields, prairie
chickens, and pray with
the rhythm of whet-stone—
shhhh, shhhh, shhhh,

bone people, melt down the bone
in savory broth, simmering
herbs, heal your broken heart—
thyme and trinity and low, low
heat to cook marrow to gold,

bone people
in the hills, dark alleys
of city noise, a quiet
tree-shadowed street, we cook,
we listen, and carry
the knife blade shine,
a glint in our eyes—
shhhh, shhhh, shhhh.

Stuck in Traffic

We are automatons who have learned to waltz
and roll, tumbling from the sky, and into traffic
that rumbles, honks, screams—looks over these fault
lines that we perch on in dazed panic,
like fragile birds huddled and hopeless together.
The wire popping with electric conversations
of shadows who meet down below and feather
nests of cogs and copper pipes, wooden slats, insulation
from cold, blazing flesh speckled with stars.
We fly, fading iridescent black and blues into haze
of greens, greys, and tailpipe exhaust from broken cars
that still grumble, stuck for a moment in a jam and maze
that city planners scribbled before they knew such machines
would rule the landscape, take us captive by routine.

What Brings Her Ghost Back

I learned to forgive the night sky
because she did not save me
from a mother who could not love,
no matter how many stars I counted,
diamonds in the blue, my forevers forgotten.
No curses. No dancing on her grave
as she did on her mother's before.

Instead, I turned from her ashes and flew
down the highway to rangelands. Dancing
on the hopes of my children's laughter.
But sometimes, baking bread at midnight,
wedging knife into the oak-topped table,
beating the soft dough with barefists,
queen of the eyesores and unwept dreams,
I remember how she shaped fragile loaves,

a childhood rising and rising again, turning sour:
3-D glasses, red and blue, Shark Week,
the smell of cheap lipstick, home perms,
and never enoughs. The ghosts that linger
in my kitchen, hissing while I bite
my lip and wait for her to dissolve
back into the dishwater and swirl down
the slow drain.
A local priest said he could not
exorcise her from our home,

not until every trace of her body was burned.
Ashes aren't enough. She's in every mirror.
Sage and fire and prayer. Three times around
smoke clearing the air. But I can still hear
her laughter. It follows me in the voice
of my daughters and sons. Love me. Forgive me.
Love me. I'm sorry. Love me.

Crawfish Étouffée

This is a main dish in the Cajun cuisine
When I was little we used to catch
crawdads in the stream by my house
You start with a roux base
I kept them as pets
Flour and butter and the holy trinity
We lived in Colorado where my mom was from
Onion, Celery, Bell Pepper I think
When we used to live in Louisiana
something bad happened
This goes in everything
My dad worked on the oilrigs
off shore a week on and a week off
Then add the other stuff
We were alone with her a lot, no babysitters
The crawfish
We went to the Piggly Wiggly
that's a grocery store
Boil and simmer
My two-year-old brother fell
out of the cart on his head
Did I forget to mention?
He stopped breathing
and his head was bleeding bright red
You got to cook the crawfish before you put it in
My mother screamed
call an ambulance!
but no one called
It has to be cooked a certain way
People in the other lines turned
their backs to us and whispered "Yankee"
You got to drop the live crawfish into a pot of high boiling water
One lady came over and got my brother
breathing again and then left
before we could thank her
So it dies instantly
Oh God he's gonna die

my mother sobbed
won't anybody help

If it dies slow or in the bathtub

She scooped him up and carried him
to the car then to the hospital
They wouldn't admit him, said take him
home to die but he lived

Its body becomes poisonous

Whenever someone dies
someone else makes a big vat
of Crawfish Étouffée
for the funeral after
for the family after

Head to toe

I can't swallow it
It smells like death to me.

Murmuration of Starfall

The universe is committing suicide in my attic—
dive bombing into buckets that fill with rainwater,
jamming the starfalls into window panes
and cracking glass. Starlings swing down,
beating their complaints against the timber
rafts, confused—*the sky was just open and now?*
Cobwebs and splinters drape them—
Where is the out, escape, escape
light that leads them back to the wind,
to the updrafts and other songs?

Sweetlings beat their wings until bones crack,
others press and press through slivered gaps,
hopeful that this may be a drought hole
and others forlorn find the buckets,
that catch the roof leaks still and stale
water mixed with guano and dust,
plunge their bodies to the bottom, hold down
drowning, drowning, in six inches of water.

The map of the universe,
patterned on their feathered backs,
murmur the secrets of God.
They call our our names sometimes
clear as day, *Hey you—Hey you—Liar—*
up the attic stairs, thrusting
and frantic, blaring like car horns
and firetrucks, from the beaks of tiny birds—
Hey you—You—Where did the sky fall?

Melting Comb Wax For Baba Yaga

Working the tool, sharp edge round the corners,
saw saw down again until the frame, glued
by wax and spit, come loose and her fingers grasp and lift,
Vasilisa hides her mother's doll from curious neighbors.
Remembering animated buzz of neglect and acrimony,
her tiny doll blade scrapes what remains into the bucket,
the wax flakes, buzzing through window sills,
dripping walls with honey, she strokes
down and down, comb curling off the wood frame.
Scavengers buzz, stealing what's left of honey in comb.
Wasps, mostly. Delicate bodice, stingers dancing,
mouths gaped. They see her doll as a thief too, and she is.
Veil and gloved, she blows with mouth fire to deep clean
each wrinkle and crack. Hold up. Inspect the frame.
Honey droplets capped in an arch over a dark sweet
center where the brood hatched, blackened now and empty.
The sharp scent warm and sticky.

Red Beaded Gumbo Prayers

Red like the Mardi Gras beads that turn
under my fingers. Father brought
them home from a bar on Bourbon Street.
I wrap them around my head, body, and dance
across the carport. Red like the garnet rosary beads
nailed over her bed to warn spirits away,
poker-playing demons that taunt her from the corner,
feufollet blinking in the darkness when she closes her eyes.
Chicken and andouille gumbo boils,
cracks through her mother's aluminum pot, cracks
breaks into the flames, fills with smoke, blood tomatoes
washing over white enamel. Red, like her rage.
Mother Mary Full of Grace, Protect us from her
battered lace. Red. Red. Red and lovely, scared
and curled on the kitchen floor, pregnant
with her third, fourth, if you count the one
never born, red, spilled and sticky on the floor.

Grace

Even in the dark,
when your hands run over my body,
this scarred message,
ink and knife pricked deep in flesh,
spins a symbol of July,
stars, mermaids drowning on dry shores,
bleached bones rolled white on the sand.

When you slide into tangled blue skies,
drown in eyes of aragonite and breathe cinnamon hair,

counting all the ways you should not love me,
this message carved in flesh,
old as stardust,
will remind you of home.

In the dark, when you wake in an eclipse of blue,
shadow of white breast and shoulder
leaning at your side,
you'll remember the last time we ended,
I was humming.

Glacial Remains
for Holly

One thousand, twenty miles inland in a field sown
with soy and corn, fish bones and sea shells, glacial
pond fossils shimmer mica in July's morning mirage.

Mermaid bones, my daughter says, tracing
smooth, white ossein, blue-green fish scales, shards
so far from the salty embrace of sea, buried

under mildew-grey silage, turning copper to water,
delicate shale. A tingle quilts my clammy flesh, brined
in sweat, a memory of whales. Wet toes curl

in my boots. *So far from home* she says, *mermaids die.*

Broken Tractor

I don't understand poetry, he said. *It is just random,*
poorly punctuated. Too simple is this: the flutter
of the sparrow's wing, the way the wind shushes the storm,
maple leaves when they are set on sweetness and fire,
the hum of the radio, late night wrenches and jacks.
Poets know about luck and sharp-scented kerosene in jars
stored on the north wall, near grimey engine rags.
Consonants stick in the gears, transmission seized hard.
These words give black coffee to the dead, pause and slice
into fresh bread, spread butter and last fall's ripe blackberries,
the glass of almost sour milk on the split oak table, the buzzing of flies.
My suitcase, fallen by the door, car keys imprinting my left sleeve.
Say something, I want to not crumble like grist.
What good are endstops and line breaks in this?

We forget too easily
what we've consumed before

The root
spreads through loose soil,
down into the cold rock,

seeking water, cool loess,
relief from harsh winds, harsher sun,

growing thick stalk, tough leaves
to stand against

falling in the storm—
for we may never get back up—

if we fall in the storm.
If we dare to lay down,

so continue to stand against,
growing thick stalk and tough leaves,

seek water, coolness,
down into the cold rock below,

the oldest living things in the world,
we've consumed before.

Walk in the Woods

Where we pull apart
what clings to us
dreams unwoven
picked and carded through
rolling in our palms each lock
to tease out what's left as it crumbles
clumps of dark soil
old parchment
like leaves
left in the rain
to dry swept up
in the wind
and like torn
confetti glitters
the sky
with words
letters
ink
strokes
then

gone.

Where Light Gets In

Dust motes dance in
beams of sunlight,
warms the wood,

your breath on me

like a river flows
over rocks, pebbles,
cools and washes
me clean.

Night falls. Let me.
The sounds of the day too much,
they corner me,
like a prizefighter, I cover my ears,

back into the dark corner
where the Milky Way spins overhead,

and your breath slows and holds

until morning brings sleep

and you. . . .or... and I . . . .

Sunshine at Night

A baritone *in the timber line,*
in the darkness,
something echoes between the trees.

A phantom in a flood
in the tall grass,
something rustles through the night.

An Irish goodbye
in the grand tradition,
something like a whisper with no warning.

Just gone.
No letter left behind.
No firm handshake,

no blood trail *in the woods.*
In the shooting stars
that once lit up the new moon sky

and then left us
in the shadows
of nothing but our lingering guilt.

Heart Math

I choose to love this time for once
with all my intelligence. —Adrienne Rich

And so   this is what I do.
I take my body   out of the equation,
out of your hands   untangle the sheets.

I stick to poems,   dreams and daily chores,
the lives of my children,   and dinner recipes,
walk the concrete sidewalks
through the neat rows of houses,

keep off the dangerous path,

                                                            wild brambles, thorny
                                                            reaches of this tension,

where dry creek beds

                                                            remember rain,
                                                            flash floods that tear
                                                            the soil from its banks.
                                                            A lustful pull that tugs
                                                            when I touch finger to lips

I tell you—be quiet, this time, not yet.

It's better to feel pain,   this heart pull,
than to burn down our homes

for the sake of   a night of sweets,
our hearts   matching rhythms,
                                 rushing waves, music,
rage and power   that ebbs and recedes,
fist clenching,
dizzy, panic, and terror.

Why this can never happen:
We drive minivans,

pick up children
from practices and lessons
make salad
for the neighborhood
potluck

                exchange glances, shy, eyes meet
                we are undone in our own heads
                in a glance, a fleeting touch of your arm

while we laugh about pie
crust and jello, and PTA meetings—
we know. We know what is at risk,
an analysis of loss.

We know,   we know.

Collapse

If bees had bones,
would I reconstruct skeletons to fuzzy
                  curiosities?
Wear them like earrings?
                      Buzzing in and out,
around my earlobes,
        tied to delicate strings.
Would they   leave
fossils in the stone of earth
so I could   remember
long after they are all
gone?   If bees had bones
would they still need   money?
Would they tickle each petal,
licking sap and pollen dust
from silk and strand,
combing the debris for evidence?
Would I be so careless
as to break them? If bees
had bones would they dance
        cupped in my hands, caught,
humming, looking for a gap in my fingers?
Would we   still
be so careful with each
other, tasting honey
with each   syllable   spilled
like kisses, stained,
fractured, splintered, jaggered
bones, this   busted lip,
this   shattering cheekbone, this
impossible collapse, this
sweetness, crunching of bones
in my honeycomb,
tasting each tooth,
each a song, each note
swallowed
        hard, stinging in my throat.

Dead Reckoning:

Part 3

Lithopedion

Wondering what poem
I had written in the night
and then forgotten. I opened
the poem called Salt.

But the page was blank.
White salt. Ildith's fate.
I had hoped for some wisdom
in our blood, of the salt

or the tears that come from the sea,
memory of ocean waves,
a pinch thrown over my shoulder
when the shaker spilled

on my grandmother's doorstep.
To keep the demons out.
But it never worked
motherhood turned her.

Then the seventies: Drugs, drink,
free love…. Is this what happens
when your oldest daughter, in a dress white
as salt, marries a pedophile?

When your seven-year-old son
dies from bedwetting?
When your own daughters hate you?
What won't save us is salt.

A possession passed down like recipes
or handmedown sheets we twist
and turn, fabric ripping and tearing
until we're left wrinkled, stained,

cupid bow lips, painted orange, stuck
with rim salt: margaritas, music,

dancing in the kitchen—
where grandmother drowned.

We become more than fingers
that roll out salt dough,
sew buttons—tear at flesh—
sometimes our own, streaked with salt.

White. Like sugar. I accidentally
spooned it into mother's tea.
Someone whispered *poison*, and she turned
into the demon we feared. Salt.

Everyday was covered with furious
grey crayon scribbles on a Monet.
Maybe no one notices it's ruined?
Maybe it isn't really salt.

Salt could never work that kind of magic.
This briny miracle on my tongue
reminds me of caramels
and the beach and brokenhearted years.

When Grandma died and her daughters danced
on her grave, I thought, *This is no place for dancing.*
You risk her reaching up through
the dirt and pulling us all in.

Maybe, maybe she already has,
if dancing is what we're all called to do
on a night like this. The page was blank
because, maybe, these things must go unsaid.

No Christmas dinner talk, this: Pass the salt.
We stare in the mirror before the painted
faces go on. Pick at wounds in the dark.
Maybe that's why I sprinkle

on my own doorstep with sea salt,
to keep from falling on the ice, from sliding
off the road, from letting go.

In navigation, dead reckoning

is the process of calculating
our current position

Currently, we are lost.
A forest fire outside Dayton, Wyoming
closed the pass and sent
us off the highway,

by using a previously determined
position, or fix, and advancing

the landscape hazy, smoke
rolling down the mountainside
the wilderness burning,

that position based upon known
or estimated speeds over
elapsed time and course

and neither of us wants to say.
We sit quietly as the road
passes steady under the tires
and the falling rocks sound like hail.

In navigation, dead reckoning
is the process of calculating
our current position.

We are strangers in this new geography.
Words tucked in pockets.
True North whispered into silence,
a false lie once followed sends us off course.

Currently we are lost.
The perfectly cut grass,
chipped white fences, graffitied
crayon scribbles and lipstick stains.

In navigation, dead reckoning
is the process of calculating
our current position.

We have calculated, balanced
checkbooks, bleary-eyed, through
coffee and diesel fuel
trying to make sense of lands,
topography neither wants to see.
We sit, still,
under half-burnt cedar trees,
their falling cracks and moans.

Currently we are lost.
The ancient landscape where stars fell,
set the mountainside on fire
is now far
behind us.

But neither wants to say,
Currently, we are lost.

Ballast

little deaths every night
la petite mort at the hands and limbs
of a competent quivering

breaks into the layer of time
from concentric intensity
signal the speed up the slow down
swallows at her feet
breakage fragments
echo and imitates laughter

but not quite

look for the darkness
the things that make our belly itch
unsettle us
bring our mind to bear
on our looking back
so both the child and the now
are glaring at us
glacier withdraws
    distraught melts nightmare

there is no graveyard here
no bones
no flesh
no buttons or hair

just the full weight of the world brought down on us
in this moment
when we dare to touch
and show what the child doesn't know
bring this darkness down on the fairytale
the measure prolonged
glides to the other side

there is no graveyard here

no bones
no flesh
no rivets or threads

just this small excuse
just these little deaths

Ash Mother

Nothing's left to devour,
with morning dew—
all night until, finally soothed
burning, curling, raging
the last sigh of a barn fire,
smoke across a prairie,
ash spilling from her throat—
whispers my desires:
in twisted knots, she rises—
sunset twirled
hair, grey with hints
long and braided—
a woman wrinkling
to my feet where
stretches
of winter's grass
turn to greenstitched
quilts and the skylight above,
sweeping blackness in
a cold cathedral of stars
above rustling grassland—
humming a homestead lullaby,
grocery lists and prayers,
rattling off
dream's haze,
I drift into a half—

If Gravity....

Not cultivated, this
in between space.

Not forgotten either.

Here's a shoe.
A dead racoon.

        A piece of muffler. The smell of diesel residue.

              Two diet soda cans,
a wristwatch, and
          what's left of someone's

taxes from 2007.

Welcome to Gravity, Iowa
        the sign says.

The shade from that sign
grows the grass a little
greener, a little less crisp.
I'm less brittle now too,
worn in the middle and at the edges,
lines from nostrils flaring
and folds from falling
down in the dirt
and I find myself in this place
where all the debris and waste is forgotten.
What happens when Gravity goes?

Daughter of the Osmanthus River

Walking in the woods,
the path I have always known,
my footing betrayed me.
I grabbed for balance,
my hands found a Honey Locust limb
to break my fall.

Pain steals my breath,
two-inch thorns pierce through flesh
puncture to bone and tendon, I let go,
pulling out as I let go,
blood pours from palm,
stigmata, betrayal.

I lie on the dry grass and stone,
tears spilled into hands,
down my shirt, mixing with the blood,
as I wrap a kerchief around the wounds,
plucking the quills and spines,
the heartbeat skipped
with each pulled thorn.

Then I think of you,
leaving debris in wounds
burying betrayal under my flesh,
working deep into my story.
This tale that haunts my days:
each thorn, opening a lingering wound,
that will never scar,
I dig with a pocket knife,
the steel blade, wet with blood-iron,
slipping in the flow, pulsing with my own
salty brine.

Drowning in a coastless ocean,
the Midwest sea of poisoned
grasslands, golden stalks

the hunters prey on with Columbines,
their harvesters, late at night, tearing
the flesh of the fields that could feed us.

My tears, like spring floods,
that try to wash away the ammonia
and waste from the topsoil, only drive
it deep into rock and water,
trapping us like rising tides on the sea wall.

Now lost. Hurt. Missing my lover—
I have named you Honey Locust.
Want to feel alive without you,
digging deep into this garden.
Want to thrive and grow
without breeding my own thorns
to keep you from my flesh.

Dredging the Lake

Unable to kick free of rusty
chains, algae, snapping turtle traps, tangled
bones, shell, and bull-head catfish sludge,
I stumble through frozen water,

strain at ropes and netting
hard enough to raise water,
churning mud, fish caught in undertow.
The old Ford, half-sunk beneath

the surface, breaks loose
a piece of door, bumper. A seam
unwelded. A seat cushion, thrashed,
rotting, rises to the surface, the rest

settles back to bottom.
I drop the lines as sunlight thaws the ice,
kaleidoscopes green and gold.
The old pull too strong.

In spring, fisherman drop new traps.
They too will soon be forgotten.
Water has a way of eating
machines. And desire.

Four Words
for Isaac

I'm lost in the words
at the tip of my tongue,
in the folds of my skirt,
pulling at my hand
when I'm cooking,
wanting something,
as the soup scorches
smelling of burned
beans and carrots,
celery, onions, and red
peppers. Holy trinity.

On the floor, I sing,
hand sign, *I love you*,
fly airplanes,
drive trains to break
through your silence.
I would give you my words
as I have given you my heart.
Hear these four words:
Mother, son, love, and loved.
You hear. Your hands shake
trying to remember, arms
gesturing in wide circles,
babbling in the language
of the silent, quick desperate
love. I am giving you words, here,
this is all I have. Take it,
right now take all of me.

I'll tell you

we're never ready for winter. Never
enough firewood cut, hay put up.
Pipes freeze. Milk cow's udders freeze
when they collapse under the weight of cold.

I know cold. Know the silent sleeping house,
the quiet of pasture on a windless day, of bloodshed
and dead calves. The children watch me from the window,

standing in the storm, alone, holding up Rosie's head;
ice slicing through my clothes, now soaked and frozen
to my skin. Ice holds her to ground.

The dark freezes the rain, prairie grass whistling
in the sharp-scented wind. I'm breathless
as my limbs ache, buckle under weight of meat, bones,
milk, blood, and cud. Boots slip in cow shit and mud.

Come on girl, I whisper.
Don't give up. Gloves soaked, fingers bleeding. We're never
ready for winter.

Kept

I.

I wake and see the bees at the window
looking in, tapping on the glass.
In the winter, I boil up sugar and water for them.
Without it they might starve, because I am a thief
and stole from them their winter food.
Contrition in simple syrup and a mason jar.

I enter the bee yard, quiet in the snow,
each footstep crunches my trail into the ice.

II.

The hives are warm, humming. The lid stuck
tight. The hive blade pulls and pries
until the lid gives with a pop.
I set the warm syrup into the top frame and square the lid back.
Winds are coming tonight, a couple bricks secure the box
Bergamot and honey stain my tongue.
Even now, I keep their nectar from them.

Last summer's stinger is still embedded in my flesh,
too deep to dig out.

III.

Sometimes I tell people, I am kept by bees
not the other way around.

They fill the gaps in my brood box, tend
the garden out back. But under magnification,
a bee's stinger makes a sewing needle look dull,
a thin dagger next to my clumsy butter knife,
feathered and barbed,

that slides in, smooth, and anchors
the pulled heart when she dies.

IV.

I wake up cold this morning. Spring sap flowing.
Stinger still throbbing under flesh.

This is how I will die. No one believes me.
It will work itself out.
Your body has a way of shutting it all down.
The bee didn't intend to hurt you like that.
Bees will be bees. What did you expect?
Where were your gloves, your suit?
You can't just work with bees wearing jeans.
They won't believe I was stung in my own bed,
children sleeping down the hall.
Now, at night I lock the door, but bees catch
in my hair, tangle in the sheets.
Tomorrow the stinger may slip into my veins and go
right for my heart. Or linger, dig deeper down to bone.

Truce

"....salt air, whose soft persistent breath
turns iron red, brass brown, and copper dull;"
—John Updike: Enemies of a House

Dry rot intruding, deeper,
moving up from below,
and *where the wood is wet*
....each line read,
the sounds gouging—rising
into a place I had forgotten
the words for—below
the cellar, in the attic,
on the oak timbered and cracked
kitchen table—his words spill
like salt and tender, flutter
on my arm, and waiting to nibble
away—a single moth lands on
what I kept folded, hung
in dark closets, tucked under
tight made beds, tied with satin—
whose soft persistent breath....
splintering, stealing from me this loss,
love will chisel these words silver,
each syllable blessed, tangled, and raw,
into the wood grain, a uneven heart,
and know better than most—regret,
Pine-Sol, and mothballs are no use
against *adultery, drink, and death.*

Milovat (Czech, v. *to love*)
for my daughters

Mockingbirds fall
from my throat, caught
for a moment, trying to fly
from where all my words
for you seem to nest,
crack from shell, and let go—

Milovat, with an ocean
between us, let this remind
you that we saved the city once
from burning. The swans,
feathers on fire, fell
out of the sky—*milovat*,
another land's song fills
empty space.

Know, I held enough
to fill a lifetime of holding
silence, and words sliding
damp down my throat,
swallowing sediment and feathers,
chasing truth until it turned,
caught me up
in angry claws.

But, too, standing on this edge,
the *most*[1] bearing weight,
a grey heron in the reed bed,
sticks, collected love letters,
egret down, a feast of slippery fish—
milovat, sweet daughters,
may you know this bird too.

[1] "Most" is bridge in Czech.

Etymology of Whale-Fish and Grace

That *H.* makes up the significance. Sets it apart from,
Wail—a broken heart or a grieving mother's grace
and *Wale*, the weft of cloth or the mark on my bosom
from the anger I made, a belt in his handsome fist.
The *gunwale* of the ship out in the Savannah harbor,
the rough planking grain of wood, salted upright.
I will not lose myself to slaking seas, drowned and blind—
this cry, swelling up from down there, this place where
only waves have known, the whale-fish and now me—
that unpronounced *H.* swallows ships and regrets and intentions,
tallow under skin for candles we burn end to end sweetly.
Wail, Wale, Whale tangle up on our flesh-eating tongues,
taking to sea before I lose myself again and again—
with each breath, I know how much that whispered *H.* is worth.

Monsters and Mouthfeel

Monsters and mayhem lurk in the closet
of my memories, whomping reptilian tails
against old clothes, grunting, rustling, shifting
to get comfortable in the cramped space
of regrets, shelved ambitions.

Sometimes I walk through woodlands,
dark as night in the day, cool even in July heat.
Nightmares peek out from behind timbers
as I stomp through, avoid sinkholes, mudfalls,
frightening beasts, large and small
with curses, fists swinging, onion patch weeds
clinging to my dirt-sweat, angry shirt,

and howl, *Ow, ow, oooooowooooo!*
Sometimes, I wish the tongues
of skinny-faced, gossiping
women were eaten by parasitic mouth leeches,
that everyone who followed them ate bad sushi,
turned inside out, begging for death's release.

But it isn't enough: rage, hatred, vengeance.
Instead, I fall, dig at the forest floor.
There, there, the creatures whisper. *Shhhhhhhh.*
Dig deeper. Find the salt of the earth,
place it to our lips and drink.
They hum and coo until
my breathing slows, the thrumming
in my heavy chest no longer
a djembe, or a jacked-up car bass.
Light dances in the cool green of the trees.
Panthers retreat. I am not for mating.
Alligators collect my tears.
Shadows fade into branches.
Willow trees shimmer and light the way.

I smile and laugh and pretend
words cannot break me.

Making Black

Lampblack, streaks on my cheeks, soot in my hair
Carbon dating this grief, dried salt and dusty air
Vine Black, define mourning as the time just after night
Graphite scribbles, on the chairs and table top, sheet music
Coals still burning under ash, still smouldering under glass
Ivory Black still in the bottle. Still in the jar. Still.
Acetylene Black, like a torch. A chemical burn.
Benzol Black, that fancy name for the crud under fingernails
Blue Black, her hair in the picture, to go with her blue shoes.
Drop Black, drop it. Just drop it. Shut. Up.
Sugar house black, sweet crust on the edge of the pan.
Can you take it back? The burned part? The crisp?
The oil slick out back has rainbows, in the black and the water.
Wine Dark. Stained. When it all. Turns. Down. Shhhh.
Ask the firewatcher. Ask her. There is no absolution.
Just a blacker black when the bones give up the smoke.

fire ants

remember the smell of flesh
when the air is hot and wet
mixed with mud and fire ants
bitter and salty like the ocean
only farther offshore

remember home
the air always smells strange

remember Louisiana winters
that cold wet breath cannot warm
bare ground and old leaves
and browns and greens
and rain that grinds
like a mean *Ssshhhhh*

foot cut on a broken beer bottle
someone left in the grass
leave little barefooted prints in blood
across the carport slip on the steps
up to the backdoor

remember her
pulling at the handle to get in
find someone to help

remember a time
when I wasn't walking through blood
with fire ants filling in the footprints

Girl

To the girl who ran barefoot through the darkness,
the woodsman said, *What of wolves, child?*

What of alligators, beasts? What of men?
The girl smiled and skipped ahead wild,

loose hair catching breezes, the woodsman dreamed,
enchanted, scent of earth rising damp, fallen leaves

while beasts of timber, breasts swollen, rumbled,
heart beat, bare bellies growling with hunger,

and lust for blood. *We were never afraid.*
We run swamp water through our veins

and bones, darkness kissing flesh, whispering desires
through branches and shadows and almost-dead fire.

The path more rugged, his urge
to protect her from the darkness merged

deeper into the woods she waltzed, one, two, three...
one, two, three...one, two, three...go.

He led the pace, she danced along. Nightfall, she
slowed and matched his step, swirling, twirling,

spinning, her eyes lit up. She turned, jaw unhinged,
tongue thrusted, swallowed deeply. *We were never afraid.*

BIOGRAPHY

Danèlle Lejeune was born in the Rocky Mountains to a hippie mother and a skydiving, Cajun father. Her family hopped around the Midwest and finally landed in Iowa (much too cold for her Southern-tinged Cajun blood). After college, she dedicated herself to motherhood, beekeeping, raising pigs, sheep and cows, and practicing the art of cooking. In 2014, she decided to attend the Ossabaw Island Writers' Retreat to research and write about pigs. Instead, she rediscovered her childhood love of poetry, quit the Iowa farm, bought an 1875 pre-Victorian home in Georgia and took up writing poetry as her life. She believes in God, Pluto's planetary status, and is curious about Earth's second moon. Lejeune's art photography has appeared online at *Flyway: Journal of Writing & Environment* and in the *Portland Review*. Her writing has been published in *Fifth Wednesday Review, Red Paint Hill, Red River Review, Nottingham Review, Whale Road Review, MothersAlwaysWrite, Glass Poetry Journal*, and *Rose Red Review*.

www.ingramcontent.com/pod-product-compliance
Lightning Source LLC
Chambersburg PA
CBHW021157090426
42740CB00008B/1136